STEP-BY-STEP

Quick & Easy Indian Cooking

Quick & Easy Indian Cooking

LOUISE STEELE

||| •PARRAGON• |||

First published in Great Britain in 1994 by
Parragon Book Service Ltd
Unit 13-17, Avonbridge Trading Estate
Atlantic Road
Avonmouth
Bristol BS11 9QD

ISBN 1 85813 624 5

Printed in Italy

Acknowledgements:

Design & DTP: Pedro & Frances Prá-Lopez / Kingfisher Design
Art Direction: Clive Hayball
Managing Editor: Alexa Stace
Special Photography: Amanda Hayward
Home Economist: Nicola Fowler
Stylist: Marion Price

Gas Hob supplied by New World Domestic Appliances Ltd
Photographs on pages 6, 18, 30, 52 & 64: By courtesy of ZEFA

Note:
Cup measurements in this book are for American cups. Tablespoons are assumed to be 15ml.

Contents

✺

CHAPTER ONE

Starters

Whether you are planning a full-scale dinner party, an informal buffet or a nourishing family meal, don't forget to include a starter or a few appetisers to tempt the tastebuds at the start of the meal. Starters or hors d'oeuvres are not generally served as such on the Indian menu, but dishes like chicken tikka, tiger prawns or spicy mini kebabs make for a typical beginning. Use hot spices cautiously in such palate-enticing dishes, and serve with a yogurt and cucumber cool dipping sauce.

Alternatively, do as the Indians do and serve a selection of snack foods like bhajis and pakoras before the main meal - they are perfect finger food to serve with drinks.

Rarely are soups served at an authentic meal – they are not considered to be traditional Indian cuisine: they are something the Indians have copied from the English since the days of the Raj.

Opposite: *A bustling scene at Crawford Market in Bombay.*

STEP 1

STEP 2

STEP 4

STEP 5

PRAWN (SHRIMP) POORIS

Tiger prawns (shrimp) are especially good cooked this way, although the less expensive, smaller peeled prawns (shrimp) may be used instead.

SERVES 6

POORIS:
60 g/2 oz/¹/₂ cup plain wholemeal flour
60 g/2 oz/¹/₂ cup plain white flour
1 tbsp ghee or vegetable oil
2 good pinches of salt
75 ml/3 fl oz/¹/₃ cup hot water

TOPPING:
250 g/8 oz fresh spinach, washed and stalks
    trimmed
4 tbsp ghee or vegetable oil, plus extra oil for
    shallow frying
1 onion, peeled and chopped
1 garlic clove, peeled and crushed
¹/₂-1 tsp minced chilli (from a jar)
1-1¹/₂ tbsp medium curry paste, to taste
250 g/8 oz canned chopped tomatoes
150 ml/¹/₄ pint/²/₃ cup coconut milk
250 g/8 oz peeled tiger prawns (shrimp)

1 To make the pooris, put the flours in a bowl and make a well in the centre. Add the ghee or oil, salt and hot water and mix to form a dough. Leave to stand for 1 hour.

2 Meanwhile, prepare the topping. Cut the spinach crossways into wide strips – do this by making bundles of leaves and slicing with a sharp knife.

3 Heat the ghee or oil in a frying pan, add the onion, garlic, chilli and spinach and cook gently for 4 minutes, shaking the pan and stirring frequently. Add the curry paste, tomatoes and coconut milk and simmer for 10 minutes, stirring occasionally. Remove from the heat, stir in the prawns (shrimp) and season with salt to taste.

4 Knead the dough well on a floured surface, divide into 6 pieces and shape into 6 balls. Roll out each one to a 12 cm/5 in round. Heat about 2.5 cm/1 in oil in a deep frying pan until smoking hot. Take one poori at a time, lower into the hot oil and cook for 10-15 seconds on each side until puffed up and golden. Remove the poori with a slotted spoon, drain on absorbent paper towels and keep warm while cooking the remainder in the same way.

5 Reheat the prawn (shrimp) mixture, stirring until piping hot. Arrange a poori on each serving plate and spoon the prawn (shrimp) and spinach mixture on to each one. Serve immediately.

STEP 1

STEP 2

STEP 3

STEP 4

SPICY CHICKEN TIKKA

Arrange these tasty kebabs on a bed of finely shredded crisp lettuce, slivered onion and grated eating apple drizzled with a little lemon or lime juice.

SERVES 6

500 g/1 lb boneless chicken breasts, skinned
salt and freshly ground black pepper
1 ½ tbsp Tikka paste (from a jar)
6 tbsp strained Greek yogurt
1 tbsp lemon juice
½ onion, peeled and finely chopped
1 ½ tbsp chopped chives or spring onion
  leaves
1 ½ tbsp finely chopped ginger root
1-2 garlic cloves, peeled and crushed
1 ½ tbsp sesame seeds
2 tbsp vegetable oil
wedges of lemon or lime, to garnish

1 Cut the chicken breasts into small bite-sized pieces, place in a shallow glass dish and season with salt and pepper to taste.

2 In a small bowl, mix together the remaining ingredients, except the sesame seeds and oil, and pour over the chicken. Mix well until all the chicken pieces are coated, then cover and refrigerate for at least 1 hour, or for longer if possible.

3 Thread the chicken pieces onto 6 bamboo or metal skewers and sprinkle with the sesame seeds.

4 Place on a rack in a grill pan and drizzle with the oil. Cook under a hot grill for about 15 minutes or until cooked through and browned, turning frequently and brushing with more oil, if necessary. Serve hot, garnished with wedges of lemon or lime.

HELPFUL HINTS

To prevent bamboo skewers charring during cooking, soak them first in cold water for 30 minutes before threading with the chicken.

MINTED ONION BHAJIS

Gram flour (also known as besan flour) is used here to make the bhajis.
It is a fine yellow flour made from ground chick peas and is readily
available from many supermarkets and Asian food shops.

STEP 1

MAKES 12

125 g/4 oz/1 cup gram flour
¹/₄ tsp cayenne pepper
¹/₄-¹/₂ tsp ground coriander
¹/₄-¹/₂ tsp ground cumin
1 tbsp chopped fresh mint
salt and freshly ground black pepper
4 tbsp strained Greek yogurt
65 ml/2¹/₂ fl oz/¹/₄ cup cold water
1 large onion, peeled, quartered and thinly
* sliced*
vegetable oil, for frying
mint sprigs, to garnish

1 Put the gram flour into a bowl, add the cayenne pepper, coriander, cumin and mint and season with salt and pepper to taste. Stir in the yogurt, water and sliced onion and mix well together.

2 One-third fill a large, deep frying pan with oil and heat until hot. Drop heaped spoonfuls of the mixture, a few at a time, into the hot oil and use two forks to neaten the mixture into rough ball-shapes.

3 Fry the bhajis until rich golden brown and cooked through, turning frequently. Drain on absorbent paper towels and keep warm while

cooking the remainder in the same way. Serve hot or warm.

STEP 2

STEP 3a

VARIATION

For a more fiery flavour, add 1 seeded and chopped fresh green chilli (or 1 teaspoon ready prepared minced chilli, from a jar) to the above ingredients and omit the cayenne pepper, if wished.

STEP 3b

STEP 1a

STEP 1b

STEP 2

STEP 3

LAMB & TOMATO KOFTAS

These little meatballs, served with a minty yogurt dressing, can be prepared well in advance, ready to cook when required.

SERVES 4

250 g/8 oz finely minced lean lamb
1½ onions, peeled
1-2 garlic cloves, peeled and crushed
1 dried red chilli, finely chopped (optional)
2-3 tsp garam masala
2 tbsp chopped fresh mint
2 tsp lemon juice
salt
2 tbsp vegetable oil
4 small tomatoes, quartered
mint sprigs, to garnish

YOGURT DRESSING:
150 ml/¼ pint/⅔ cup strained Greek
 yogurt
5 cm/2 in piece cucumber, grated
2 tbsp chopped fresh mint
½ tsp toasted cumin seeds (optional)

1 Place the minced lamb in a bowl. Finely chop 1 onion and add to the bowl with the garlic and chilli, if using. Stir in the garam masala, mint and lemon juice and season well with salt. Mix the ingredients well together. Divide the mixture in half, then divide each half into 10 equal portions and form each into a small ball. Roll balls in the oil to coat. Quarter the remaining onion half and separate into layers.

2 Thread 5 of the balls, 4 tomato quarters and some of the onion layers onto each of 4 bamboo or metal skewers. Brush the vegetables with the remaining oil and cook under a hot grill for about 10 minutes, turning frequently until they are browned all over and cooked through.

3 Meanwhile, prepare the yogurt dressing. Mix the yogurt with the cucumber, mint and toasted cumin seeds, if using. Garnish the lamb koftas with mint sprigs and serve hot with the yogurt dressing.

SHAPING KOFTAS

It is important that the lamb is finely minced and the onion finely chopped or the mixture will not shape neatly and easily into balls. The mixture could be finely processed in a food processor, if wished.

STEP 1

STEP 3

STEP 4a

STEP 4b

PAKORAS

These vegetable fritters are simple to make and extremely good to eat.
They may be served as a tasty starter or as an accompaniment
to a main course.

SERVES 4-6

125g/4 oz broccoli
1 onion
2 potatoes
175 g/6 oz/1½ cups gram flour
1 tsp garam masala
1½ tsp salt
½ tsp cayenne pepper
1 tsp cumin seeds
200 ml/7 fl oz/just under 1 cup water
vegetable oil, for deep frying
coriander sprigs, to garnish

1 Cut the broccoli into small florets, discarding most of the stalk and cook in a pan of boiling, salted water for 4 minutes. Drain well, return to the pan and shake dry over a low heat for a few moments. Place the broccoli on absorbent paper towels to completely dry while preparing the other vegetables.

2 Peel and thinly slice the onion and separate into rings. Peel and thinly slice the potatoes and pat dry.

3 Place the gram flour in a bowl with the garam masala, salt, cayenne pepper and cumin seeds. Make a well in the centre, add the water and mix to form a smooth batter.

4 One-third fill a deep fat fryer or pan with oil and heat to 190°C/375°F or until a cube of day-old bread browns in 30 seconds. Dip the vegetables into the batter to coat, then lower into the hot oil and fry, in batches, for 3-4 minutes or until golden brown and crisp. Drain on absorbent paper towels and keep warm while cooking the remainder in the same way. Serve the pakoras hot, garnished with coriander sprigs.

VARIATIONS

Small cauliflower florets, strips of red or green (bell) pepper and slices of courgette (zucchini) are also very good cooked this way. The cauliflower should be par-cooked in the same way as broccoli (see step 1) before dipping in the batter. Use up the leftover broccoli (or cauliflower) stalks in a soup, rice or main course dish.

16

CHAPTER TWO

Fish

At first glance India may not be considered to be a great fish-eating nation, but there are some parts of it, notably Bengal and around Karachi, where fish is very popular and consequently plays a very important part in the diet. Indeed India has a coastline stretching for over 2,500 miles and with internal waters can supply over 2,000 varieties of fish!

Many fish and shellfish are simply grilled, whole or on skewers, after sprinkling with a few spices and brushing with mustard oil; others are fried whole or as fish and vegetable fritters; some with a firm, meaty texture, like cod, are curried in aromatic sauces and frequently flavoured with coconut. Countless others are baked, steamed, poached or roasted with that characteristic Indian flavour that is based on a marsala of spices that enhances, but does not overwhelm, the delicate flavour of the fish.

Opposite: *Pushkar Lake, Rajasthan. Both freshwater fish and seafood play a large part in the cooking styles of India.*

STEP 1a

STEP 1b

STEP 2

STEP 3

PRAWNS (SHRIMP) & CHILLI SAUCE

Quick and easy to prepare and extremely good to eat. Use the large and succulent tiger prawns (shrimp) for special occasions.

SERVES 4

4 tbsp ghee or vegetable oil
1 onion, peeled, quartered and sliced
1 bunch spring onions (scallions), trimmed and sliced
1 garlic clove, peeled and crushed
1-2 fresh green chillies, seeded and finely chopped
2.5 cm/1 in piece ginger root, finely chopped
1 tsp ground turmeric
1 tsp ground cumin
1 tsp ground coriander
1½ tsp curry powder or paste
1 x 400 g/14 oz can chopped tomatoes
150 ml/¼ pint/⅔ cup water
150 ml/¼ pint/⅔ cup double (heavy) cream
500 g/1 lb peeled prawns (shrimp)
1-2 tbsp chopped fresh coriander
salt
coriander sprigs, to garnish

1 Heat the ghee or vegetable oil in a saucepan and fry the onions, garlic and chilli over gentle heat for 3 minutes. Stir in the ginger, spices and curry powder or paste and cook very gently for a further 1 minute, stirring all the time.

2 Stir in the tomatoes and water and bring to the boil, stirring. Reduce the heat and simmer for 10 minutes, stirring occasionally.

3 Add the cream, mix well and simmer for 5 minutes, then add the prawns (shrimp) and coriander and season with salt to taste. Cook gently for 2-3 minutes. Taste and adjust the seasoning, if necessary. Serve garnished with coriander sprigs.

PREPARING EARLY

This dish may be prepared in advance to the end of step 2. A few minutes before the dish is required for serving, reheat the mixture until simmering then follow the instructions given in step 3.

INDIAN GRILLED TROUT

Here is a deliciously simple way of preparing and cooking trout.
It is also good with nice fresh, plump mackerel.

STEP 1

SERVES 4

4 trout, each weighing about 250 g/8 oz,
   cleaned
salt
6 tbsp ghee or melted butter
1-2 garlic cloves, peeled and crushed
1 fresh green chilli, seeded and chopped, or
   use 1 tsp minced chilli (from a jar)
2.5 cm/1 in ginger root, peeled and finely
   chopped
1½ tsp cumin seeds
1 tsp garam masala
1 tsp ground cumin
finely grated rind of 1 lemon
juice of 2 lemons
coriander sprigs and lemon wedges, to
   garnish

1 Using a sharp knife, carefully make 3 diagonal slashes (not too deep) on each side of the trout. Season the trout and place in a lightly greased grill (broiler) pan.

2 Heat the ghee or butter in a small pan over a low heat, add the crushed garlic, chilli, chopped ginger and spices and cook very gently for 30 seconds, stirring. Remove the pan from the heat and stir the lemon rind and juice into the mixture.

3 Spoon half the mixture over the trout and cook under a moderately hot grill (broiler) for 5-8 minutes or until cooked on one side. Turn the fish over and spoon the remaining mixture over the fish and grill (broil) for a further 5-8 minutes, basting with the juices in pan during cooking.

4 Arrange the trout on a hot serving plate, spoon the pan juices over the fish and garnish with coriander sprigs and lemon wedges. Serve hot.

STEP 2a

STEP 2b

SLASHING THE TROUT

Take care when making the diagonal slashes on either side of the trout not to cut too deeply or you will cut into the bones and spoil the finished result.

STEP 3

STEP 1

STEP 2

STEP 3

STEP 4

SPICY FISH & POTATO FRITTERS

*You need nice, floury-textured old (main crop) potatoes for making
these tasty fritters. Any white fish of your choice may be used.*

SERVES 4

*500 g/ 1 lb potatoes, peeled and cut into
even-sized pieces
500g/ 1 lb white fish fillets, such as cod or
haddock, skinned and boned
6 spring onions (scallions), sliced
1 fresh green chilli, seeded
2 garlic cloves, peeled
1 tsp salt
1 tbsp medium or hot curry paste
2 eggs, beaten
150 g/ 5 oz/ 2½ cups fresh white
breadcrumbs
vegetable oil, for shallow frying
mango chutney, to serve
lime wedges and coriander sprigs, to garnish*

1 Cook the potatoes in a pan of
boiling, salted water until tender.
Drain well, return the potatoes to the pan
and place over a moderate heat for a few
moments to dry off. Cool slightly, then
place in a food processor with the fish,
onions, chilli, garlic, salt and curry paste.
Process until the ingredients are very
finely chopped and blended.

2 Turn the potato mixture into a
bowl and mix in 2 tablespoons of
beaten egg and 60 g/ 2 oz/ 1 cup of
breadcrumbs. Place the remaining

beaten egg and breadcrumbs in separate
dishes.

3 Divide the fish mixture into 8 and,
using a spoon to help you (the
mixture is quite soft), dip first in the
beaten egg and then coat in the
breadcrumbs, and carefully shape the
mixture into ovals.

4 Heat enough oil in a large frying
pan for shallow frying and fry the
fritters over moderate heat for 3-4
minutes, turning frequently, until golden
brown and cooked through. Drain on
absorbent paper towels and garnish with
lime wedges and coriander sprigs. Serve
hot, with mango chutney.

FRITTERS

Make these fish fritters more or less fiery
by increasing or reducing the amount of
chilli, as wished. For really speedy fritters,
simply drop spoonfuls of the egg and
crumbed fish mixture into the hot fat and
using a palette knife, pat into rough
shapes during cooking.

SEAFOOD & AROMATIC RICE

One of those easy, delicious meals where the rice and fish are cooked together in one pan. The whole spices are not meant to be eaten: they are there to flavour the dish during cooking and are removed before serving.

STEP 1

Serves 4

250 g/8 oz/1¼ cups basmati rice
2 tbsp ghee or vegetable oil
1 onion, peeled and chopped
1 garlic clove, peeled and crushed
1 tsp cumin seeds
½-1 tsp chilli powder
4 cloves
1 cinnamon stick or a piece of cassia bark
2 tsp curry paste
250 g/8 oz peeled prawns (shrimp)
500g/1 lb white fish fillets (such as
    monkfish, cod or haddock), skinned and
    boned and cut into bite-sized pieces
salt and freshly ground black pepper
600 ml/1 pint/2½ cups boiling water
60 g/2 oz/⅓ cup frozen peas
60 g/2 oz/⅓ cup frozen sweetcorn kernels
1-2 tbsp lime juice
2 tbsp toasted desiccated (shredded) coconut
coriander sprigs and lime slices, to garnish

1 Place the rice in a sieve and wash well under cold running water until the water runs clear, then drain well. Heat the ghee or oil in a saucepan, add the onion, garlic, spices and curry paste and fry very gently for 1 minute.

2 Stir in the rice and mix well until coated in the spiced oil. Add the

prawns (shrimp) and white fish and season well with salt and pepper. Stir lightly, then pour in the boiling water.

3 Cover and cook gently for 10 minutes, without uncovering the pan. Add the peas and corn, cover and continue cooking for a further 8 minutes. Remove from the heat and allow to stand for 10 minutes.

4 Uncover the pan, fluff up the rice with a fork and transfer to a warm serving platter. Sprinkle the dish with the lime juice and toasted coconut, and serve garnished with coriander sprigs and lime slices.

STEP 2

STEP 3

VARIATION

For yellow rice, add ½ teaspoon ground turmeric to the pan together with the other spices at step 1. Alternatively, to add flavour as well as colour to the dish, omit the turmeric and instead add 2 good pinches of toasted and crushed saffron strands.

STEP 4

STEP 1

STEP 2

STEP 3a

STEP 3b

INDIAN COD WITH TOMATOES

Quick and easy – cod steaks are cooked in a rich tomato and coconut sauce to produce tender, succulent results. You can, of course, use any firm white fish available instead of cod.

SERVES 4

3 tbsp vegetable oil
4 cod steaks, about 2.5 cm/1 in thick
salt and freshly ground black pepper
1 onion, peeled and finely chopped
2 garlic cloves, peeled and crushed
1 red (bell) pepper, seeded and chopped
1 tsp ground coriander
1 tsp ground cumin
1 tsp ground turmeric
½ tsp garam masala
1 x 400 g/14 oz can chopped tomatoes
150 ml/¼ pint/⅔ cup coconut milk
1-2 tbsp chopped fresh coriander or parsley

1 Heat the oil in a frying pan, add the fish steaks, season with salt and pepper and fry until browned on both sides (but not cooked through). Remove from the pan and reserve.

2 Add the onion, garlic, red (bell) pepper and spices and cook very gently for 2 minutes, stirring frequently. Add the tomatoes, bring to the boil and simmer for 5 minutes.

3 Add the fish steaks to the pan and simmer gently for 8 minutes or until the fish is cooked through. Remove from the pan and keep warm on a serving dish. Add the coconut milk and coriander to the pan and reheat gently. Spoon the sauce over the cod steaks and serve immediately.

VARIATIONS

The mixture may be flavoured with a tablespoonful of curry powder or curry paste (mild, medium or hot, according to personal preference) instead of the mixture of spices at step 2, if wished.

CHAPTER THREE

Meat & Poultry

Curries are, of course, the most famous of the Indian meat dishes, but they are by no means the only dishes the Indian culinary repertoire has to offer! Consider stir-fries with a blend of Indian spices, skewered kebabs of meat and vegetables, vegetables stuffed with savoury meat and rice or lentil mixtures, risotto-style combinations of meat with rice, or meat roasted tandoori-style.

Even then there are differences and variations which give a typical national dish a distinctive regional flavour all of its own. South Indian curries, for example, are fierce and fiery, while North Kashmiri and Punjab meat dishes are mild and strongly flavoured with onion and garlic. Western or Goan dishes are slow-cooked, hot and thickened with coconut milk, whereas Eastern meat dishes rely upon spices like mustard, cumin and anise for their distinctive flavour and originality.

Opposite: *Unloading supplies on the banks of the Ganges, in the holy city of Benares.*

STEP 1a

STEP 1b

STEP 2a

STEP 2b

CHICKEN WITH SPICY CHICK-PEAS

This is a delicious combination of chick-peas and chicken flavoured with fragrant spices. Using canned chick-peas (rather than the dried ones) speeds up the cooking time considerably.

SERVES 4

3 tbsp ghee or vegetable oil
8 small chicken portions, such as thighs or
    drumsticks
1 large onion, peeled and chopped
2 garlic cloves, peeled and crushed
1-2 fresh green chillies, seeded and chopped,
    or use 1-2 tsp minced chilli (from a jar)
2 tsp ground cumin
2 tsp ground coriander
1 tsp garam masala
1 tsp ground turmeric
1 x 425 g/14 oz can chopped tomatoes
150 ml/¼ pint/⅔ cup water
1 tbsp chopped fresh mint
1 x 475 g/15 oz can chick-peas, drained
salt
1 tbsp chopped fresh coriander
natural yogurt, to serve (optional)

1 Heat the ghee or oil in a large saucepan and fry the chicken pieces all over until sealed and lightly golden. Remove from the pan. Add the onion, garlic, chilli and spices and cook very gently for 2 minutes, stirring frequently.

2 Stir in the tomatoes, water, mint and chick-peas. Mix well, return the chicken portions to the pan, season with salt to taste, then cover and simmer gently for about 20 minutes or until the chicken is tender and cooked through.

3 Taste and adjust the seasoning if necessary, then sprinkle with the chopped coriander and serve hot, drizzled with yogurt, if using.

VARIATIONS

Canned black-eyed beans and red kidney beans also make delicious additions to this spicy chicken dish. Be sure to drain the canned beans and to rinse them, if necessary, before adding to the pan.

STEP 1

STEP 2a

STEP 2b

STEP 3

CHICKEN IN SPICED COCONUT

*This delicious combination would make a perfect dinner or supper
party course – and what's more it is quick and simple to prepare.*

SERVES 4

4 boneless chicken breasts, skinned
6 tbsp vegetable oil
2 onions, peeled, quartered and thinly sliced
1 garlic clove, peeled and crushed
*2.5 cm/1 in fresh ginger root, peeled and
    finely chopped*
*1-2 fresh green chillies, seeded and finely
    chopped, or use 1-2 tsp minced chilli (in a
    jar)*
175 g/6 oz mushrooms, wiped and sliced
2 tsp medium curry powder
2 tsp ground coriander
1/2 tsp ground cinnamon
1 tbsp sesame seeds
*150 ml/1/4 pint/2/3 cup chicken stock or
    water*
1 x 250 g/8 oz can chopped tomatoes
300 ml/1/2 pint/1 1/4 cups coconut milk
salt
coriander sprigs, to garnish

1 Cut each chicken breast into 3
diagonal pieces. Heat 4 tablespoons
of oil in a saucepan and fry the chicken
pieces until lightly sealed all over.
Remove from the pan and reserve.

2 Add the remaining oil to the pan
and gently fry the onions, garlic,
ginger, chillies, mushrooms, curry

powders, spices and sesame seeds for 3
minutes, stirring frequently. Stir in the
chicken stock, tomatoes and coconut
milk. Season with salt to taste and bring
to the boil.

3 Reduce the heat, return the
chicken pieces to the pan and
simmer gently, uncovered, for about 12
minutes, or until the chicken is tender
and cooked through and the sauce has
thickened, stirring occasionally. Garnish
with coriander sprigs.

SPICES

Increase the pungency of the mixture by
adding more curry powder or chilli, to
taste. You can also leave the dish to stand
overnight to allow the flavours to develop
and reheat it gently when required.

CHICKEN & AROMATIC ALMONDS

Rich and delicious – enjoy the succulence of chicken cooked with yogurt, cream and ground almonds flavoured with aromatic garam masala.

STEP 1

SERVES 4

150 ml/¹/₄ pint/²/₃ cup strained Greek yogurt
¹/₂ tsp cornflour (cornstarch)
4 tbsp ghee or vegetable oil
4 boneless chicken breasts
2 onions, peeled and sliced
1 garlic clove, peeled and crushed
2.5 cm/1 in piece fresh root ginger, peeled and chopped
1¹/₂ tbsp garam masala
¹/₂ tsp chilli powder
2 tsp medium curry paste
300 ml/¹/₂ pint/1¹/₄ cups chicken stock
salt and freshly ground black pepper
150 ml/¹/₄ pint/²/₃ cup double (heavy) cream
60 g/2 oz/¹/₂ cup ground almonds
125 g/4 oz French green beans, topped, tailed and halved
juice of ¹/₂ lemon
toasted flaked almonds, to garnish
boiled rice, to serve

1 Smoothly blend the yogurt in a small bowl with the cornflour (cornstarch). Heat the ghee or oil in a large flameproof casserole, add the chicken breasts and fry until golden all over. Remove the chicken from the casserole and reserve.

2 Add the onions, garlic and ginger to the casserole and fry gently for 3 minutes, then add the garam masala, chilli powder and curry paste and fry gently for 1 minute. Stir in the stock, yogurt and salt and pepper to taste and bring to the boil, stirring all the time.

3 Return the chicken breasts to the casserole, then cover and simmer gently for 25 minutes. Remove the chicken to a dish and keep warm.

4 Blend the cream with the ground almonds and add to the sauce, then stir in the green beans and lemon juice and boil vigorously for 1 minute, stirring all the time.

5 Return the chicken to the casserole, cover and cook gently for a further 10 minutes. Serve with rice and garnish with toasted flaked almonds.

ALTERNATIVE

Chicken portions may be used instead of breasts, if preferred, and should be cooked for 10 minutes longer at step 3.

STEP 2

STEP 4

STEP 5

STEP 1

STEP 2

STEP 3

STEP 4

STIR-FRY CHICKEN CURRY

A tasty mix of chicken, peppers and cashew nuts is stir-fried with spices to give a delicious dish in minutes.

SERVES 4

4 boneless chicken breasts, skinned
6 tbsp strained Greek yogurt
juice of 1 lime
2 garlic cloves, peeled and crushed
5 cm/2 in piece ginger root, peeled and
  chopped
2 tbsp medium or hot curry paste, to taste
1 tbsp paprika
salt
5 tbsp ghee or vegetable oil
1 onion, peeled, quartered and separated into
  layers
1 red (bell) pepper, seeded and cut into
  1 cm/^{1}/$_2$ in pieces
1 green (bell) pepper, seeded and cut into 1
  cm/^{1}/$_2$ in pieces
60 g/2 oz/^{1}/$_2$ cup unsalted cashews
4 tbsp water
snipped chives or spring onion (scallion)
  leaves, to garnish

1 Cut the chicken breasts into 1 cm/^{1}/$_2$ in wide strips and place in a bowl. Add the yogurt, lime juice, garlic, ginger, curry paste and paprika. Season well and mix the ingredients together.

2 Heat the ghee or oil in a large frying pan, add the onion, red and green (bell) pepper and the cashews and stir-fry over a moderate heat for 2 minutes. Remove from the pan and reserve.

3 Stir the chicken mixture into the pan and stir-fry for 4-5 minutes until well sealed and cooked though.

4 Add the water and mix well, then return the vegetables to the pan, reduce the heat and cook gently for 2 minutes. Serve at once, sprinkled with chives or spring onion (scallion) leaves.

VARIATIONS

Thin strips of pork tenderloin or rump steak are also extremely good cooked this way. Add slices of courgette (zuccini) or celery instead of one of the (bell) peppers, if wished, and substitute blanched almonds for the cashews.

STEP 1

STEP 3a

STEP 3b

STEP 4

CHICKEN & VEGETABLE RICE

Boneless chicken breasts may be used here instead of the drumsticks, if preferred, in which case slash them diagonally through the skin and into the flesh to allow the flavours of the sauce to penetrate.

SERVES 4-6

4 chicken drumsticks
3 tbsp mango chutney
1½ tbsp lemon juice
6 tbsp vegetable oil
1½-2 tbsp medium or hot curry paste
1½ tsp paprika
1 large onion, peeled and chopped
2 garlic cloves, peeled and crushed
125 g/4 oz button mushrooms, wiped and
   left whole
2 carrots, peeled and thinly sliced
2 celery sticks, trimmed and thinly sliced
½ aubergine (eggplant), quartered and sliced
½ tsp ground cinnamon
250 g/8 oz/1¼ cups long-grain rice
600 ml/1 pint/2½ cups chicken stock or
   water
60 g/2 oz frozen peas or sliced green beans
60 g/2 oz/⅓ cup seedless raisins
salt and freshly ground black pepper
wedges of hard-boiled egg and lemon slices,
   to garnish (optional)

1 Slash the drumsticks twice on each side, cutting through the skin and deep into the flesh each time. Mix the chutney with the lemon juice,1 tablespoon oil, curry paste and paprika. Brush over the drumsticks and reserve the remainder for later.

2 Heat 2 tablespoons of oil in the frying pan and fry the drumsticks over a moderate heat for about 5 minutes until sealed and golden brown all over.

3 Meanwhile, heat the remaining oil in a saucepan, add the onion, mushrooms, carrots, celery, aubergine (eggplant), garlic and cinnamon and fry lightly for 1 minute. Stir in the rice and cook gently for 1 minute, stirring until the rice is well coated with the oil. Add the stock and the remaining mango chutney mixture, peas, raisins and salt and pepper to taste. Mix well and bring to the boil.

4 Reduce the heat and add the drumsticks to the mixture, pushing them down into the liquid. Cover and cook gently for 25 minutes until the liquid has been absorbed, the drumsticks are tender and the rice is cooked.

5 Remove the drumsticks from the pan and keep warm. Fluff up the rice mixture and transfer to a warm serving plate. Arrange the rice into a nicely shaped mound and place the drumsticks around it. Garnish the dish with wedges of hard-boiled egg and lemon slices, if using.

BEEF & MUSHROOM CURRY

*Vary the meat here according to personal taste, using lean lamb or pork
(leg or shoulder cuts are ideal) instead of beef. Omit the
finishing touches, see step 4, if wished.*

STEP 1

SERVES 4

750 g/1¹/₂ lb lean braising beef, trimmed
3 tbsp vegetable oil
2 onions, peeled, quartered and sliced
2 garlic cloves, peeled and crushed
*2.5 cm/1 in piece ginger root, peeled and
    chopped*
*2 fresh green chillies, seeded and chopped, or
    use 1-2 tsp minced chilli (from a jar)*
1¹/₂ tbsp medium curry paste
1 tsp ground coriander
*175-250 g/6-8 oz mushrooms, thickly
    sliced*
900 ml/1¹/₂ pints/3¹/₂ cups stock or water
3 tomatoes, chopped
¹/₂-1 tsp salt
60 g/2 oz creamed coconut, chopped
2 tbsp ground almonds

TO FINISH:
2 tbsp vegetable oil
*1 green or red (bell) pepper, seeded and cut
    into thin strips*
*6 spring onions (scallions), trimmed and
    sliced*
1 tsp cumin seeds

1 Cut the beef into small bite-sized
cubes. Heat the oil in a saucepan,
add the beef and fry until sealed, stirring
frequently. Remove from the pan.

2 Add the onions, garlic, ginger,
chillies, curry paste and coriander
to the pan and cook gently for 2 minutes.
Stir in the mushrooms, stock and
tomatoes and season with salt to taste.
Return the beef to the pan, then cover
and simmer very gently for 1¼-1½ hours
or until beef is tender.

3 Stir the chopped creamed coconut
and ground almonds into the
curry, then cover the pan and cook
gently for 3 minutes.

4 Meanwhile, heat the remaining oil
in a frying pan, add the (bell)
pepper strips and spring onion (scallion)
slices and fry gently until glistening and
tender-crisp. Stir in the cumin seeds and
fry gently for 30 seconds, then spoon the
mixture over the curry and serve at once.

STEP 2

STEP 3

PREPARATION

You will find this dish is even tastier if
made the day before as this allows time
for the flavours to blend and develop.
Make the curry to the end of step 3, cool
and store in the refrigerator until required.
Reheat it gently until piping hot before
adding the finishing touches.

STEP 4

STEP 1

STEP 2

STEP 3

STEP 4

PORK CHOPS & SPICY RED BEANS

*A tasty and substantial dish that is packed full of goodness. The spicy
bean mixture, served on its own, also makes a good accompaniment
to meat or chicken dishes.*

SERVES 4

3 tbsp ghee or vegetable oil
4 pork chops, rind removed
2 onions, peeled and thinly sliced
2 garlic cloves, peeled and crushed
2 fresh green chillies, seeded and chopped or
    use 1-2 tsp minced chilli (from a jar)
2.5 cm/1 in piece ginger root, peeled and
    chopped
1¹/₂ tsp cumin seeds
1¹/₂ tsp ground coriander
600 ml/1 pint/2¹/₂ cups stock or water
2 tbsp tomato purée (paste)
¹/₂ aubergine (eggplant), trimmed and cut
    into 1 cm/¹/₂ in dice
salt
1 x 439 g/14 oz can red kidney beans,
    drained
4 tbsp double (heavy) cream
sprigs of coriander, to garnish

1 Heat the ghee or oil in a large
frying pan, add the pork chops and
fry until sealed and browned on both
sides. Remove from the pan and reserve.

2 Add the sliced onions, garlic,
chillies, ginger and spices and fry
gently for 2 minutes. Stir in the stock,
tomato purée (paste), aubergine
(eggplant) and salt to taste.

3 Bring the mixture to the boil, place
the chops on top, then cover and
simmer gently over medium heat for 30
minutes, or until the chops are tender
and cooked through.

4 Remove the chops for a moment
and stir the red kidney beans and
cream into the mixture. Return the chops
to the pan, cover and heat through
gently for 5 minutes. Taste and adjust
the seasoning, if necessary. Serve hot,
garnished with coriander sprigs.

VARIATIONS

Use lamb chops instead of pork chops, if
wished. Canned chick-peas and black-
eyed beans are also delicious cooked this
way in place of the red kidney beans
(remember to drain them first before
adding to the pan).

STEP 1

STEP 2a

STEP 2b

STEP 3

LAMB & POTATO MASALA

It's so easy to create delicious Indian dishes at home – simply open a can of curry sauce, add a few interesting ingredients and you have a splendid dish that is sure to be popular with family or friends.

SERVES 4

750 g/ 1 ½ lb lean lamb (from the leg)
4 tbsp ghee or vegetable oil
500 g/ 1 lb potatoes, peeled and cut in large
  2.5 cm/ 1 in pieces
1 large onion, peeled, quartered and sliced
2 garlic cloves, peeled and crushed
175 g/ 6 oz mushrooms, thickly sliced
1 x 283 g/ 10 oz can Tikka Masala Curry
  Sauce
300 ml/ ½ pint/ 1 ¼ cups water
salt
3 tomatoes, halved and cut into thin slices
125 g/ 4 oz spinach, washed and stalks
  trimmed
sprigs of mint, to garnish

1 Cut the lamb into 2.5 cm/ 1 in cubes. Heat the ghee or oil in a large pan, add the lamb and fry over moderate heat for 3 minutes or until sealed all over. Remove from the pan.

2 Add the potatoes, onion, garlic and mushrooms and fry for 3-4 minutes, stirring frequently. Stir the curry sauce and water into the pan, add the lamb, mix well and season with salt to taste. Cover and cook very gently for 1 hour or until the lamb is tender and cooked through, stirring occasionally.

3 Add the sliced tomatoes and the spinach to the pan, pushing the leaves well down into the mixture, then cover and cook for a further 10 minutes until the spinach is cooked and tender. Garnish with mint sprigs and serve hot.

SPINACH LEAVES

Spinach leaves wilt quickly during cooking, so if the leaves are young and tender add them whole to the mixture; larger leaves may be coarsely shredded, if wished, before adding to the pan.

STEP 1

STEP 3

STEP 4a

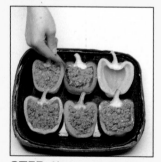

STEP 4b

(BELL) PEPPERS WITH LAMB

This colourful dish can be prepared in advance, ready to cook in the oven when required. Minced beef, pork or chicken can be instead of the lamb, if wished.

SERVES 4-6
OVEN:190°C/375°F/GAS 5

4 tbsp vegetable oil
500 g/1 lb lean minced lamb
2 onions, peeled and finely chopped
2 garlic cloves, peeled and crushed
3.5cm/1½ in ginger root, peeled and finely
chopped
2 tsp minced chilli (from a jar)
1 tsp ground coriander
1 tsp ground cumin
4 tbsp strained Greek yogurt
2 tbsp tomato purée (paste)
2 tbsp chopped fresh mint
90 g/3 oz frozen peas
1 x 227 g/8 oz can chopped tomatoes
salt and freshly ground black pepper
3 large red (bell) peppers
sprigs of mint, to garnish

1 Heat 3 tablespoons of oil in a saucepan, add the lamb and fry until sealed all over. Stir in the onions, garlic, ginger, chilli and spices and cook gently for 5 minutes.

2 Stir in the yogurt, tomato purée (paste), mint, peas, tomatoes and seasoning to taste. Cover and cook gently for 15 minutes, stirring frequently. Place in the preheated oven.

3 Meanwhile, cut the (bell) peppers in half lengthways, cutting through the stalks and leaving them attached. Scoop out the seeds and membranes from each one. Add the (bell) pepper halves to a pan of boiling water and simmer for 5-7 minutes or until only just tender – take care not to overcook. Drain well, refresh with cold water and drain well again. Pat dry on absorbent paper towels.

4 Brush the (bell) peppers with the remaining oil and arrange in a shallow, greased ovenproof dish. Spoon the lamb mixture into the (bell) peppers. Cover with greased foil and cook in the oven for 15-20 minutes until piping hot. Serve hot, garnished with mint sprigs.

(BELL) PEPPERS

A mixture of red, yellow and orange (bell) peppers really does look most attractive – giving a hot and fiery appearance. If necessaary, to keep the filled pepper halves steady in the ovenproof dish during cooking, place them on crumpled kitchen foil.

SPICY BEEF & YOGURT

Deliciously quick and easy – stir-fried steak is served with a tangy aubergine (eggplant) yogurt dressing. Use mild, medium or hot curry paste according to taste.

STEP 1

SERVES 4

500 g/1 lb lean rump steak, trimmed
4 tbsp ghee or vegetable oil
2 onions, peeled and sliced
2 garlic cloves, peeled and crushed
2 tbsp mild, medium or hot curry paste
1 tsp minced chilli (from a jar)
150 ml/¹/₄ pint/²/₃ cup beef stock
1 x 227 g/8 oz can chopped tomatoes

AUBERGINE (EGGPLANT) YOGURT:
¹/₂ medium aubergine (eggplant)
150 ml/¹/₄ pint/²/₃ cup strained Greek yogurt
1 garlic clove, peeled and crushed
1 tbsp chopped fresh coriander or parsley
salt and freshly ground black pepper

1 First make the Aubergine (Eggplant) Yogurt. Peel the aubergine (eggplant) and cut into 2.5 cm/1 in pieces. Place in the top half of a steamer and steam over boiling water for 10 minutes.

2 Meanwhile, whisk the yogurt with the garlic, coriander and salt and pepper to taste. Allow the cooked aubergine (eggplant) to cool slightly, then mash with a fork. Stir the aubergine (eggplant) into the yogurt.

3 Heat the ghee or oil in a large frying pan, add the beef and onions and stir-fry for 5 minutes until the beef is sealed all over.

4 Stir in the garlic, curry paste, chilli, stock and tomatoes and bring to the boil. Cover, reduce the heat and simmer gently for 5 minutes, stirring occasionally. Serve hot with the aubergine (eggplant) yogurt.

STEP 2

STEP 3

VARIATIONS

You could use thin strips of pork tenderloin or chicken breast instead of the rump steak, if preferred, and serve with Raita rather than Aubergine (Eggplant) Yogurt, for a change: see recipe on page 76.

STEP 4

CHAPTER FOUR

Accompaniments

No Indian-style meal is complete without a bowl of fluffy Basmati rice, a mixed vegetable side dish (often curried), spicy lentils or at the very least a small bowl of natural yogurt with some diced fruit and vegetables like cucumber, carrot, banana, tomato and onion, often flavoured with herbs like mint and coriander.

Delicately-scented Basmati rice, enhanced with the flavour of mild spices, makes the standard accompaniment, but to ring the changes consider coconut rice with its richer and more distinctive coconut flavouring. Mixed vegetable bhajis lend extra variety to a meal as do potatoes cooked with typically Indian spices.

These extras all contribute to give an Indian meal extra flavour and texture. Supplement them with a wide range of ready-made breads like poppadoms, Naan bread (plain or spiced) and stuffed samosas, not forgetting fruity relishes like mango, cooling sauces like Cucumber Raita and pickles with a kick, like lime.

Opposite: Chilli peppers drying. Chillies are frequently used in Indian cooking, but be careful to remove the seeds unless you like your food very hot indeed.

STEP 1

STEP 2

STEP 3

STEP 4

AROMATIC PILAU

This rice dish forms the perfect accompaniment to most main courses. It can be prepared ahead of time and reheated in the microwave oven just before serving.

SERVES 4-5

250 g/8 oz/1¼ cups basmati rice
2 tbsp ghee or vegetable oil
1 onion, peeled and chopped
3 cardamom pods, crushed
3 black peppercorns
3 cloves
1 tsp cumin seeds
½ cinnamon stick or piece of cassia bark
½ tsp ground turmeric
600 ml/1 pint/2½ cups boiling water or stock
60 g/2 oz/⅓ cup seedless raisins or sultanas
60 g/2 oz frozen peas
30 g/1 oz/¼ cup toasted, flaked almonds
crisp fried onion rings, to garnish (optional)

1 Place the rice in a sieve and wash well under cold running water until the water runs clear. Drain well.

2 Heat the oil in a large saucepan, add the onion and spices and fry gently for 1 minute, stirring all the time. Stir in the rice and mix well until coated in the spiced oil, then add the boiling water or stock and season with salt and pepper to taste.

3 Bring to the boil, stir well, then cover, reduce the heat and cook gently for 15 minutes without uncovering. Add the raisins and peas, re-cover and leave to stand for 15 minutes.

4 Uncover, fluff up with a fork and stir the toasted flaked almonds into the mixture. Serve hot, garnished with crisp fried onion rings, if liked.

SPICES

The whole spices used for flavouring the rice are not meant to be eaten and may be removed from the mixture, if wished, before serving. Simply double up the quantities given for serving 8-10 portions for a party.

STEP 1

STEP 2a

STEP 2b

STEP 3

DAL WITH SPINACH

Continental lentils are cooked in a delicious blend of spinach, onion, garlic and spices. Okra, also known as bhindi or ladies' fingers, are a favourite vegetable in Indian cooking.

SERVES 4

250 g/8 oz/1 cup continental lentils
1.25 litres/2 pints/5 cups water
6 tbsp vegetable oil
1 large onion, peeled and chopped
1 leek, trimmed and shredded
350 g/12 oz spinach, stalks trimmed and
*   leaves coarsely shredded*
1 red (bell) pepper, seeded and chopped
2-3 garlic cloves, peeled and crushed
1-2 tsp minced chilli (from a jar)
1¹/₂-2 tsp cumin seeds
1¹/₂-2 tsp ground coriander
salt and freshly ground black pepper
mango chutney, to serve

1 Place the lentils in a sieve and rinse well under cold running water. Drain, then place in a saucepan with the water. Cover and cook for 30 minutes until the lentils are tender and the liquid has been absorbed.

2 Meanwhile, heat the oil in a large saucepan and add the chopped onion, leek, shredded spinach and red (bell) pepper. Fry gently for 8 minutes, stirring and turning frequently until the spinach has wilted. Stir in the garlic, chilli and spices and fry gently for a further 2 minutes.

3 When the lentils are cooked, uncover and shake the pan over a moderate heat for a few moments to dry off. Add the lentils to the saucepan containing the spinach and onion mixture and toss together. Season with salt and pepper to taste and serve hot, with mango chutney.

SPINACH

Fresh spinach is used in this recipe, although frozen leaf spinach (not chopped) may be used instead if more convenient. You require 250g/8 oz frozen spinach, and it should be thawed and squeezed dry before using.

SPICY INDIAN-STYLE POTATOES

Potatoes cooked this way are so delicious, yet quick and simple to prepare. Cut the potatoes into similar-sized pieces to make sure they cook evenly.

STEP 1

SERVES 4

750 g/1½ lb potatoes
salt
60 g/2 oz/¼ cup ghee or butter
2 tbsp vegetable oil
1 tsp ground turmeric
1 large onion, peeled, quartered and sliced
2-3 garlic cloves, peeled and crushed
5 cm/2 in piece ginger root, peeled and chopped
1½ tsp cumin seeds
¼-½ tsp cayenne pepper
2 tsp lemon juice
1 tbsp shredded mint leaves
sprigs of mint, to garnish

1 Peel the potatoes and cut into 2-2.5 cm/¾-1 in cubes and cook in a pan of boiling, salted water for 6-8 minutes or until knife-tip tender (do not overcook). Drain well, return to the pan and shake dry over a moderate heat for a few moments.

2 Heat the ghee or butter and oil in a large frying pan over medium heat. Stir in the turmeric, then add the sliced onion and the cooked potatoes and fry for 4-5 minutes or until the mixture is beginning to brown, stirring and turning the vegetables frequently.

3 Stir in the garlic, ginger, cumin seeds, cayenne and salt to taste. Fry over gentle heat for 1 minute, stirring all the time.

4 Transfer the potatoes to a warm serving dish. Add the lemon juice to the juices in the pan and spoon the mixture over the potatoes. Sprinkle with the shredded mint leaves, garnish with sprigs of mint and serve hot.

STEP 2a

STEP 2b

POTATOES

This method of cooking potatoes is perfect for using up leftover potatoes – in fact if you've time, par-boil the potatoes in advance and leave them to cool before frying for even tastier results.

STEP 4

STEP 2a

STEP 2B

STEP 3

STEP 4

COCONUT RICE

A delicious rice dish flavoured with coconut and lemon. For a luxurious touch you can fork through a few shelled, chopped pistachios at the final stage.

SERVES 4-5

250 g/8 oz/1¼ cups basmati rice
3 tbsp ghee or vegetable oil
1 onion, peeled and chopped
2 garlic cloves, peeled and crushed
2.5 cm/1 in piece ginger root, peeled and chopped
½ cinnamon stick or piece of cassia bark
2 carrots, peeled and grated
600 ml/1 pint/2½ cups boiling water or stock
salt and freshly ground black pepper
30 g/1 oz creamed coconut, finely chopped
finely grated rind of ½ lemon or 1 lime
1 tbsp chopped fresh coriander
1 bunch spring onions (scallions), trimmed and sliced

1 Place the rice in a sieve and wash well under cold running water until the water runs clear. Drain well.

2 Heat the ghee or oil in a large saucepan, add the onion, garlic, ginger and cinnamon and fry gently for 1 minute. Stir in the rice and grated carrots and mix until well coated with the oil.

3 Stir in the water or stock and season with salt and pepper. Bring to the boil, cover, reduce the heat and simmer gently for 15 minutes without taking off the lid.

4 Add the creamed coconut, lemon rind, chopped coriander and spring onions (scallions), fork through and serve immediately.

FOR A SPICIER VERSION

A little garam masala, sprinkled over the rice just before serving adds an interesting "warm" spiciness to this rice dish. If a more fiery flavour is required, fork a little slivered fresh chilli (or minced chilli from a jar) through the rice at step 4.

MIXED VEGETABLE BHAJI

In this delicious dish, the vegetables are first par-boiled and then lightly braised with onions, tomatoes and spices.

STEP 1a

SERVES 4-6

1 small cauliflower
125 g/4 oz French green beans
2 potatoes
4 tbsp ghee or vegetable oil
1 onion, peeled and chopped
2 garlic cloves, peeled and crushed
5 cm/2 in ginger root, peeled and cut into
    fine slivers
1 tsp cumin seeds
2 tbsp medium curry paste
1 x 425 g/14 oz can chopped tomatoes
150 ml/¼ pint/⅔ cup water
4 tbsp strained Greek yogurt
chopped fresh coriander, to garnish

1 Break the cauliflower into neat florets. Top, tail and halve the beans. Peel and quarter the potatoes lengthways, then cut each quarter into 3 pieces. Cook all the prepared vegetables in a pan of boiling, salted water for 8 minutes. Drain the vegetables well, return to the pan and shake dry over a low heat for a few moments.

2 Heat the ghee or oil in a large frying pan, add the onion, garlic, ginger and cumin seeds and stir-fry gently for 3 minutes. Stir in the curry paste, tomatoes and water and bring to

the boil. Reduce the heat and simmer the spicy mixture for 2 minutes.

3 Stir in the par-cooked vegetables and mix lightly. Cover and cook gently for 5-8 minutes until just tender and cooked through. Whisk the yogurt to soften and drizzle the vegetable mixture with the yogurt. Sprinkle with the chopped coriander. Serve hot.

STEP 1b

STEP 2

POTATO ALTERNATIVES

New potatoes are ideal for this dish as they have a more waxy texture and retain their shape better than old (main crop) potatoes which, when overcooked, become floury and lose their shape. You could use turnip or pumpkin instead of potatoes, if preferred.

STEP 3

CHAPTER FIVE

Desserts

Indian-style meals are traditionally rounded off with something very sweet or with a large selection of carefully prepared plain fresh fruits like mangoes, guavas, melon and pears. These are best served well chilled, especially in the summer months and can make a welcome change or contrast to a spicy, warm, aromatic main course feast. Dice, slice, or cut the fruit into colourful wedges then arrange them on a huge platter with sprigs of mint for a stunning finale to an Indian meal.

The simplest, and often most appreciated dessert is a cooling Kulfi or ice-cream. Many are served plain but others are flavoured with mango and coconut and are delicious if sprinkled with chopped shelled pistachios or almonds.

Opposite: A wide selection of delicious fruits are grown in India. Favourite desserts tend to be fresh fruit, fruit salads or ice-creams.

INDIAN ICE-CREAM (KULFI)

*To make traditional Kulfi is quite a time-consuming process,
so why not try this deliciously easy version instead?*

STEP 1

SERVES 6-8

4 cardamom pods, crushed and seeds
   removed
75 ml/ 3 fl oz/¹/₃ cup boiling water
1 x 405 g/ 14 oz can sweetened condensed
   milk
75 ml/ 3 fl oz/¹/₃ cup cold water
30 g/ 1 oz/¹/₄ cup unsalted pistachio nuts
30 g/ 1 oz/ ¹/₄ cup blanched almonds
2 drops almond essence (optional)
150 ml/¹/₄ pint/²/₃ cup double (heavy)
   cream
   lime zest and rose petals, to decorate
   (optional)

1 Pour the boiling water into a bowl,
   stir in the cardamom seeds and
leave for 15 minutes to infuse.
Meanwhile, put the condensed milk into
a blender or food processor together with
the cold water, pistachio nuts, almonds
and almond essence, if using. Process the
mixture for about 30 seconds until very
finely mixed.

2 Add the cooled and strained
   cardamom water and pour into a
bowl. Whip the cream until softly
peaking and whisk into the mixture.
Pour the mixture into a shallow metal or
plastic container and freeze for about 3

STEP 2

hours or until semi-frozen around the
edges and mushy in the centre.

3 Transfer the mixture to a bowl and
   mash well with a fork (to break up
the ice crystals). Divide the mixture
evenly between 6-8 small moulds (see
below) and freeze for at least 4 hours or
overnight until firm.

4 To serve, dip the base of each
   mould quickly into hot water and
run a knife around the top edge. Turn
out on to serving plates and decorate
with lime zest and rose petals, if using.

STEP 3a

MOULDING THE KULFI

Traditionally this dessert is frozen in
special conical-shaped moulds, but you
can use dariole moulds, small yogurt pots
or fromage frais cartons instead.

STEP 3b

STEP 1

STEP 2

STEP 3a

STEP 3b

MANGO & YOGURT CREAM

*This wonderfully refreshing dessert is designed to help refresh
the palate after a hot and spicy meal.*

SERVES 6

2 large ripe mangoes
2 tbsp lime juice
2 tbsp caster sugar
*150 ml/¹/₄ pint/²/₃ cup double (heavy)
    cream*
*150 ml/¹/₄ pint/²/₃ cup strained Greek
    yogurt*
*4 cardamom pods, crushed, and seeds
    removed and crushed*
lime twists or zest, to decorate

1 To prepare each mango, cut along either side of the large central stone, to give two halves of mango. Remove the seed, scoop out the flesh and discard the skin.

2 Place the flesh in a blender or food processor with the lime juice and sugar and process until the mixture forms a smooth purée. Turn the mixture into a bowl.

3 Whip the cream in a bowl until stiff, then fold in the yogurt and the crushed cardamom seeds. Reserve 4 tablespoons of the mango purée for decoration, and mix the remaining mango purée into the cream and yogurt mixture.

4 Spoon the mixture into pretty serving glasses. Drizzle a little of the reserved mango sauce over each dessert and serve chilled, decorated with lime twists.

MANGOES

When choosing mangoes, select ones that are shiny with unblemished skins. To test if they are ripe for eating, gently cup the mango in your hand and squeeze it gently – it should give slightly to the touch if ready for eating.

STEP 1a

STEP 1b

STEP 2a

STEP 2b

AROMATIC FRUIT SALAD

The fruits in this salad are arranged attractively on serving plates with the spicy syrup spooned over.

SERVES 6

60 g/ 1 ½ oz/ 3 tbsp granulated sugar
150 ml/ ¼ pint/ ⅔ cup water
1 cinnamon stick or large piece of cassia bark
4 cardamom pods, crushed
1 clove
juice of 1 orange
juice of 1 lime
½ honeydew melon
a good-sized wedge of watermelon
2 ripe guavas
3 ripe nectarines
about 18 strawberries
a little toasted, shredded coconut for
 sprinkling
sprigs of mint or rose petals, to decorate
strained Greek yogurt, for serving

1 First prepare the syrup. Put the sugar, water, cinnamon, cardamom pods and cloves into a pan and bring to the boil, stirring to dissolve the sugar. Simmer for 2 minutes, then remove from heat, add the orange and lime juices and leave to cool and infuse while preparing the fruits.

2 Peel and remove the seeds from the melons and cut the flesh into neat slices. Cut the guavas in half, scoop out the seeds, then peel and slice the flesh neatly. Cut the nectarines into slices and hull and slice the strawberries.

3 Arrange the slices of fruit attractively on 6 serving plates. Strain the prepared cooled syrup and spoon over the sliced fruits. Sprinkle with a little toasted coconut. Decorate each serving with sprigs of mint or rose petals and serve with yogurt, if wished.

VARIATIONS

Use any exotic fruits of your choice, or those that are in season. You can, of course, cut up the fruits and serve them in a.bowl, in the usual way, if you prefer.

STEP 2

STEP 3

STEP 4a

STEP 4b

COCONUT ICE-CREAM

This delicious ice-cream will make the perfect ending to any Indian meal. For a smooth-textured dessert leave out the coconut.

SERVES 6

150 g/ 5 oz/²/₃ cup granulated sugar
300 ml/ ¹/₂ pint/ 1 ¹/₄ cups water
2 x 400 ml/ 14 fl oz cans coconut milk
300 ml/ ¹/₂ pint/ 1 ¹/₄ cups double (heavy)
   cream
2 tbsp desiccated (shredded) coconut
sprigs of mint or rose petals, to decorate

1 Place the sugar and water in a saucepan and heat gently, stirring occasionally until the sugar dissolves. Boil gently for 10 minutes without stirring, then remove from the heat and allow to cool slightly.

2 Mix the cooled syrup with the coconut milk and pour into a shallow freezer container. Cover and freeze for about 3 hours or until semi-frozen around the edges and mushy in the centre.

3 Transfer the mixture to a bowl and cut up with a knife, then place (half the quantity at a time) in a food processor and process until smooth.

4 Turn the mixture into a bowl. Whip the cream until softly peaking and fold into the ice-cream, then stir in the desiccated coconut. Return the mixture to the container and freeze again until solid.

5 Before serving, remove the container of ice-cream to the refrigerator and leave in the main compartment for 30 minutes (or at room temperature for 15 minutes) to soften. Scoop or spoon the ice-cream into serving dishes and decorate with sprigs of mint.

SERVING ICE-CREAM

For easy serving, scoop the ice-cream into portions the night before required and place on a chilled baking tray, then freeze until ready to serve.

STEP 1

BANANAS WITH SPICED YOGURT

This simple but delicious dessert is at its nicest when made with thick and creamy strained Greek yogurt.

STEP 1a

SERVES 4-6

3 good pinches saffron strands
2 tbsp creamy milk
6 cardamom pods, crushed and seeds
   removed and crushed
45 g/ 1½ oz/ 3 tbsp butter
45 g/ 1½ oz/ 3 tbsp soft brown sugar
½ tsp ground cinnamon
2 bananas
500 g/ 1 lb strained Greek yogurt
2-3 tbsp clear honey, to taste
30 g/ 1 oz/¼ cup toasted, flaked almonds

1 Place the saffron strands on a small piece of foil and toast very lightly. Crush the saffron strands finely and place in a small bowl. Add the milk and crushed cardamom seeds, stir well and leave to cool.

2 Meanwhile, melt the butter in a frying pan, add the brown sugar and cinnamon and stir well. Peel and slice the bananas and fry gently for about 1 minute, turning halfway through cooking. Remove from the pan and place the fried banana slices in decorative serving glasses.

3 Mix the yogurt with the cold spiced milk and the honey. Spoon the

mixture on top of the bananas and liberally sprinkle the surface of each serving with toasted, flaked almonds. Chill before serving, if preferred.

STEP 2a

ALTERNATIVE

The flavour of saffron strands is improved by lightly toasting before use, but do take care not to overcook them or the flavour is spoilt and becomes bitter. This delicious dessert may also be made using half cream and half yogurt and the tops could be sprinkled with unsalted, chopped pistachios instead of almonds, if wished.

STEP 2b

INDIAN COOKING

Below is a selection of deliciously easy accompaniments to serve with your Indian dishes.

Apple and onion relish peel, core and coarsely grate 1 large cooking apple into a bowl. Add ½ bunch chopped spring onions (scallions), 2 tsp vinegar or lemon juice, 1-2 tsp caster sugar, to taste, and ½ tsp roasted cumin seeds. Mix well and chill before serving, sprinkled with chopped fresh coriander.

Radish and cucumber yogurt put 600 ml /1 pint/2½ cups natural yogurt into a bowl and season with salt and freshly ground black pepper. Stir in ½ bunch trimmed and coarsely chopped radishes, ¼ unpeeled, diced cucumber, 1 small chopped onion and 15-30 ml/ 1-2 tbsp chopped fresh mint. Serve chilled.

Cucumber raita mix 600 ml / 1 pint/2½ cups natural yogurt with ¼ peeled and grated cucumber. Season with salt, freshly ground black pepper and a pinch or two of cayenne pepper. Just before serving, dry roast 1 tsp cumin seeds, then crush coarsely and sprinkle over the yogurt mixture just before serving. Add a little finely chopped fresh mint to the mixture, if wished.

continued opposite

It's never been easier to create quick and authentic tasting Indian dishes thanks to the marvellous range of exciting spices, tempting ingredients and ready-prepared products so widely available. All the ingredients used in the recipes in this book are easy to find from the larger supermarkets.

SPICES

Spices play an essential part in Indian cooking, but don't be put off by the vast array of jars and packets on the supermarket shelves, remember that you only need a few to give characteristic flavour to your Indian cooking.

It is best to buy whole spices (they keep their flavour and aroma much longer than the ready ground spice) and to grind them as you need them. A small coffee grinder, electric mill or a pestle and mortar does the job easily. If you cook a lot of Indian dishes, it may well be worth grinding the various spices in small quantities at a time: store them in small, airtight containers and use up quickly.

When time is short, however, do make the most of the excellent range of commercially prepared products widely available in supermarkets. Spice mixtures such as curry powders, garam masala and tandoori spices and the jars of ready-made curry pastes, etc. are extremely convenient and make light work of adding flavour and authenticity to Indian-style dishes. Useful too, are the jars of ready-minced chilli and chopped

fresh ginger – and the varied selection of canned curry sauces (ranging from mild to medium and hot) ensure there is something to please most palates.

Here is a suggestion of just a handful of spices well worth buying to give your Indian meals that special flavour and aroma:

Cardamom These small pods contain numerous tiny black seeds which have a warm, highly aromatic flavour – green cardamoms are considered the best. Cardamom pods (used in savoury and sweet dishes) are often lightly crushed prior to adding to dishes to allow the full flavour of the seeds to be appreciated.

When the whole or crushed pods are used they are not meant to be eaten and should either be removed before serving or simply left on the side of the plate by the diner.

When the seeds only are required, the pods should be lightly crushed to break them open and the seeds removed for using whole or crushed, according to the recipe. Use a pestle and mortar or the end of a rolling pin for crushing either pods or seeds.

Cinnamon Available in stick and ground form. Shavings of bark from the cinnamon tree are processed and curled to form cinnamon sticks and these will keep almost indefinitely in an airtight container. This fragrant spice is used to flavour savoury and sweet dishes and drinks. The sticks are not edible and should be removed before serving, or may be used as a garnish or decoration.

Cassia Cassia comes from the bark of the cassia tree. It is not as uniform in shape as cinnamon sticks, but has a similar, less delicate flavour.

Cloves These dried unopened flower buds are used to give flavour and aroma to foods, but should be used with care as the flavour can become overpowering. When whole cloves are used they are not meant to be eaten and may be removed before serving, if wished.

Coriander An essential spice in Indian cooking, coriander has a mild and spicy flavour with a slight hint of orange peel. It is available as seeds or ground.

Cumin These caraway-like seeds are used extensively in Indian dishes either in their whole or ground form. Cumin has a warm, pungent and aromatic flavour.

Garam masala This is a ground aromatic spice mix that generally includes cardamom, cinnamon, cumin, cloves, peppercorns and nutmeg. It may be used during and towards the end of cooking, or sprinkled over dishes as an aromatic garnish just before serving. You can buy this spice ready-mixed or prepare your own quite simply: finely grind together 1 tsp each black peppercorns and cumin seeds with 1 tbsp cardamom seeds, 8 whole cloves, a 5 cm/2 in piece of cinnamon stick or cassia bark and about ¼ teaspoon freshly grated nutmeg. Store the mixture in an airtight container and use within 3 weeks. This quantity makes about 3 tablespoonfuls.

Ginger Fresh root ginger is now widely available from supermarkets and green grocers. It looks like a knobbly brown stem and should be peeled and chopped, sliced or grated before use. It is also now available ready-minced in jars.

Paprika This ground, bright red pepper, although similar in colour to fiery cayenne pepper, has a mild flavour and is used for colouring as well as flavouring dishes.

Saffron This spice (the most expensive of all) has a distinctive flavour and gives a rich yellow colouring to dishes. It is available in small packets and jars, either powdered or in strands – the strands have by far the better flavour.

Turmeric Is an aromatic root which is dried and ground to produce a bright, orangey-yellow powder. It has a warm, distinctive smell and a delicate, aromatic flavour. It is frequently used to give dishes an attractive yellow colouring.

CHILLIES

Fresh chillies, used extensively in Indian dishes to give them their hot and fiery flavour, vary considerably in size, shape and hotness – it really depends on the variety. It's worth remembering that all chillies are hot, so use caution when adding them to a dish, it is wise to start with small amounts – you can always add more to taste at a later stage

Tasty Accompaniments continued.
Carrot, raisin and onion salad coarsely grate 250g/8 oz carrots into a bowl. Peel and quarter 1 onion, cut into paper-thin slices and add to the carrots. Stir in 45 ml/3 tbsp seedless raisins and 15 ml/1 tbsp lemon juice. Season with ¼ tsp paprika, ½ tsp grated fresh ginger, salt and freshly ground black pepper. If wished, add slivers of fresh chilli (or a little minced chilli, from a jar) for a more fiery flavour. Mix all the ingredients well together and leave to stand for 30 minutes before serving, to allow time for the flavours to develop.

DRINKS

When serving spicy dishes be sure to have a supply of refreshing drinks to hand – chilled mineral water, iced water or fruit juice are excellent choices. For special occasions and for a deliciously refreshing drink to sip during a hot, spicy meal, serve iced water flavoured with spices, such as cardamom, cumin, cassia or cinnamon. Wine is not good served with Indian foods, since the taste is overpowered by the strong flavours of the food, so opt instead for chilled lagers and light beers. You could also provide a jug of Lassi – the delicious Indian drink of lightly spiced yogurt which is designed to cool the palate.

To Make Lassi: put 600 ml/1 pint/2½ cups natural yogurt in a blender or food processor with 1.5 litres/2½ pints/6¼ cups cold water, 1-2 tsp lemon juice, 15 ml/1 tbsp chopped fresh mint, ½ tsp each salt and dry-roasted cumin and freshly ground black pepper to taste. Blend for about 1 minute, then serve in a jug or tall glasses filled with crushed ice.

To Make Sweet Lassi: omit the lemon juice, mint, salt, cumin and pepper and instead flavour the yogurt and water with sugar, ground cardamom and a little rosewater, to taste. Blend well and serve over crushed ice.

according to personal preference. Take care too, when preparing chillies. The cream-coloured seeds inside are the hottest part and may be removed before using, if wished: generally, the seeds are only left in if you like your spicy dishes very hot indeed! Chillies contain a pungent oil which can cause an unpleasant burning sensation to eyes and skin, so it is advisable to wear thin polythene or rubber gloves when handling them and to be sure not to touch your face or eyes during preparation.

To prepare a chilli: cut the chilli in half lengthways, cut off the stalk end, then scrape out the seeds with a pointed knife and discard. Rinse the chilli under cold running water and pat dry before chopping or slicing as required. Once you have finished, thoroughly wash your hands, utensils and surfaces with soapy water.

Dried red chillies are sold whole or ground and are used to make cayenne pepper, chilli and curry powders. Again, remove the seeds from dried chillies. Chilli powders come in varying degrees of strength, so check the label before you buy, as many are a blend of chilli and other spices, such as "chilli seasoning" – a popular blend that is quite mild.

You can also buy ready-minced red chilli in a jar from many supermarkets – this is an excellent and most convenient way of adding a fiery touch to Indian dishes without any hassle.

Green chillies, too, are available in brine or pickled in sweetened vinegar – these should be drained and dried on paper towels before using.

FRESH CORIANDER (DHANIA)

This pretty green herb has leaves rather similar in appearance to flat-leaf parsley. It is frequently used in Indian dishes both as a garnish and for its delicate flavour.

COCONUT

Many Indian dishes are flavoured with coconut and the ready prepared desiccated (shredded) type is convenient and easy to use, however, you really do get the very best flavour from fresh grated coconut. It freezes well too, so is well worth preparing to freeze away in handy quantities to use when required.

To prepare for freezing: choose a fresh coconut that is heavy with liquid (best way to check is to give it a good shake before buying). Break it in half, drain off the liquid and prise the coconut from its shell. Using a potato peeler, peel off the brown skin and break the flesh into smallish pieces. Place in a food processor and process until finely grated, or, if preferred grate larger pieces on a cheese grater. Freeze in small usable quantities for up to 3 months. It thaws quickly and can be used as required.

Coconut milk too, is a popular ingredient in Indian cooking and is available in liquid form in cans, or as coconut milk powder in sachets, to make up into a liquid following the packet instructions.

You can also make your own delicious version very easily: chop 1 x 198 g/7 oz packet creamed coconut and place in a heatproof measuring jug. Pour in enough boiling water to come to the 600 ml/1 pint/2½ cup mark and stir until dissolved. Cool and use as required. This will keep in the refrigerator for up to 1 week.

GHEE

Indian recipes often call for ghee (or clarified butter) for cooking. It can be cooked at high temperatures without burning, gives a delicious rich, nutty flavour to all manner of dishes and a glossy sheen to sauces. You can buy ghee in cans from supermarkets and Indian food shops – and a vegetarian ghee is also available. Vegetable oil may be used instead of ghee, as preferred.

RICE

The two types of rice most frequently used in Indian cooking are long-grain rice (also called American long-grain or Patna rice) and basmati rice which, although rather more expensive, is prized for its slender grains and fine aromatic flavour. This is the one to use whenever possible, but if you can't afford this variety every time, save it for special occasions.

It is essential to rinse rice, particularly basmati, in a sieve under cold running water, before cooking to get rid of the starchy residue left from the milling process. Easy-cook rice, including basmati, is now widely available in supermarkets and always gives good results. It is also now possible to buy brown basmati rice, which will take a little longer to cook.

YOGURT

Homemade yogurt (dahi) is used extensively in Indian cooking for marinading meats and poultry to tenderise and flavour them and also as an ingredient in various dishes and sauces. It is also widely used as a cooling accompaniment to spicy dishes, such as Raita, see recipe on page 76. Strained Greek yogurt, with its tart, creamy flavour, most closely resembles the homemade yogurt eaten by Indian families. A brief whisk before using will thin the consistency, if necessary. Any natural yogurt of your choice may be used instead, if preferred.

SUPERMARKET ADDITIONS TO A HOMEMADE INDIAN MEAL

There's a wonderful selection of ready-prepared products available from supermarkets that you could include with your homemade dishes. A basket of poppadums, for example, is always favourite as a starter. Other traditional and popular accompaniments could include parathas, chapatis or naan, plus a bowl of yogurt or Raita (see above) and a selection of shop bought pickles or chutneys such as lime or mango.

DRINKS TO SERVE
You will need a supply of cooling and refreshing drinks to accompany an Indian meal – the best ones are ice-cold water, chilled lagers or beers and fruit juices. Fine wine is rather wasted since the taste is overpowered by the strong flavours of the food.

DAL

Dal are actually split peas, lentils and beans. There are several different kinds available, which can all be used to make the Dal that you will find on the menu in Indian restaurants.

250 g/8 oz chana dal or yellow split peas, soaked
1.25 litres/2 pints water
½ tsp turmeric
1 onion, chopped
1 tsp ground cumin
2 tbsp vegetable oil
½ tsp mustard seeds
2 garlic cloves, crushed
2 dried chillies, seeded and chopped
250 g/8 oz canned chopped tomatoes
salt and pepper

1. Drain and rinse the lentils then place in a pan with the water and turmeric. Bring to the boil then cover and simmer for 30 minutes.

2. Add the onion and cumin, stir, cover and cook for another 15 minutes.

3. Meanwhile, heat the oil in a small pan and add the mustard seeds. When the seeds pop add the chillies and tomatoes. Cook for 2-3 minutes then add the contents of the pan to the lentils. Stir well, add salt and pepper to taste and serve.

INDEX